THE OXFORD
EASY ANTHEM BOOK

MUSIC DEPARTMENT
OXFORD UNIVERSITY PRESS
LONDON   NEW YORK   TORONTO

THE need has long been felt in English-speaking countries for a book of easy anthems which might appeal to choirs who find some of the music in the *Church Anthem Book* beyond their powers. Accordingly the present volume consisting of fifty easy anthems has been compiled in conjunction with the Committee on Public Worship and Aids to Devotion of the General Assembly of the Church of Scotland, whose help and guidance in selection is warmly acknowledged.

Grateful thanks are due to Mr. Herrick Bunney, acting as music adviser to the Committee on Public Worship, for his valuable advice.

OXFORD UNIVERSITY PRESS
MUSIC DEPARTMENT 44 CONDUIT STREET LONDON W1R ODE

© 1957, Oxford University Press
Tenth impression 1978

Reproduced and printed by
Halstan & Co. Ltd., Amersham, Bucks., England

ALPHABETICAL INDEX

Anthems suitable for unaccompanied singing are marked thus *

INDEX OF COMPOSERS, EDITORS, AND ARRANGERS

Anthems suitable for unaccompanied singing are marked thus *
(The figures on the left refer to Anthem numbers, the figures on the right to page numbers)

★

INDEX OF ANTHEMS
SUITABLE FOR VARIOUS SEASONS AND OCCASIONS

★

1. DEAREST LORD JESU

(LIEBSTER HERR JESU)

(?) CHRISTOPH WERNER (1676)
Tr: BEATRICE E. BULMAN

Melody and figured bass by
J.S.BACH (1736)
(Ed. Charles Kennedy Scott)

Copyright, 1945, by the Oxford University Press, London.

Printed in Great Britain

Je - su, Oh why dost Thou tar-ry? oh why dost Thou tar-ry?

Je - su, Oh why dost Thou tar-ry? oh why dost Thou tar-ry?

Je - su, Oh why dost Thou tar-ry? oh why dost Thou tar-ry?

Je - su, Oh why dost Thou tar-ry? oh why dost Thou tar-ry?

Come now for I am of wait-ing so wea-ry, so—wea—ry.

Come now for I am of wait-ing so wea-ry, so wea—ry.

Come now for I am of wait-ing so wea-ry, so—wea—ry.

Come now for I am of wait-ing so wea-ry, so 'wea—ry.

4

2. COME, THOU LONG EXPECTED JESUS

CHARLES WESLEY
(1707-1788)

HENRY G. LEY

long— ex-pect-ed Je - sus, Born to set— Thy peo - ple

free,   From our fears and sins re - lease   us,   Let us   find_ our

rest_ in Thee.   Is - rael's Strength and Con - so - la - tion,

Hope of   all   the earth Thou   art,   Dear De - sire_ of eve - ry

na - tion, Joy of eve - ry long - - ing heart. ___

eve - ry long-ing heart. ___

long - - ing heart. ___

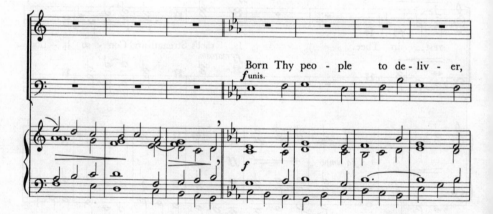

Born Thy peo - ple to de - liv - er,

Born a Child and yet__ a King,   Born to reign in us ___ for

senza Ped.

*Small notes throughout are optional.

3. CHRIST IS THE WORLD'S TRUE LIGHT

(Unison with descant)

G. W. BRIGGS   W. K. STANTON

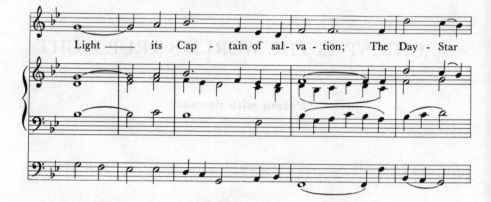

Light —— its Cap - tain of sal - va - tion; The Day - Star

clear and bright of ev - 'ry man and na - tion. New life, new

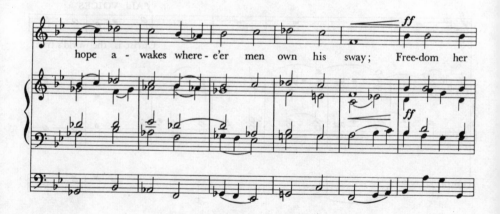

hope a - wakes where - e'er men own his sway; Free-dom her

bon - dage breaks,   and night is   turned to ___ day.

mf SOPRANO VOICES

In Christ all ___ ra - ces   meet, ___

___ their   ancient feuds   for- get - ting,   The whole round world com-

-plete,   from sun - rise   to   its   set - ting.   When Christ is   throned as

Lord, men   shall   for - sake   their   fear;   To plough-share beat the

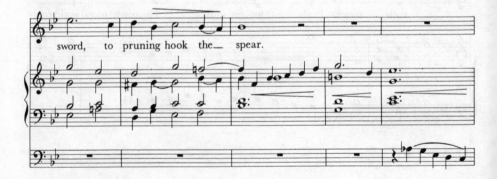

sword,   to   pruning hook the— spear.

world has wait - ed long, has tra - vailed long in pain; To

world has wait - ed long, has__ tra - vailed long in pain; To

(Pedal Reed)   (Reed off)

heal   its   an - cient wrong, Come Prince of   Peace and

heal   its an - cient wrong, Come Prince of   Peace and __

reign.

reign.

fff

4. SHEPHERDS LOUD THEIR PRAISES SINGING

(Based on the tune 'Quem Pastores')

Traditional*

ALEC ROWLEY

*With additional verses, 2 and 5, by Alec Rowley.

Copyright, 1951, by the Oxford University Press, London.

Hence all fears and sad - ness fling-ing: Born to - day— is Christ our

King.   2. Gen - tle Child, so

still— Thou sleep - eth,   Ten - der   watch   His   mo - ther   keep - eth,

O, what pains Thy love — it reap - eth, Born to - day — is

Christ our King.

3. Kings to meet Him

forth are far - ing, Gold, frank-in - cense — and myrrh pre - par - ing:

Straight all to the man - ger bear - ing; Born to - day— is

Christ our King.   4. Lo! the star o'er Bethl - 'em

stay - eth: Heaven's own light— the Child ar - ray - eth: Peace on

Peace

earth, good - will— be - wray - eth: Born— to - day— is   Christ our

on   earth, ———   Born   to - day   is   Christ our

King.   5. Son   of   God,   the   earth— a -

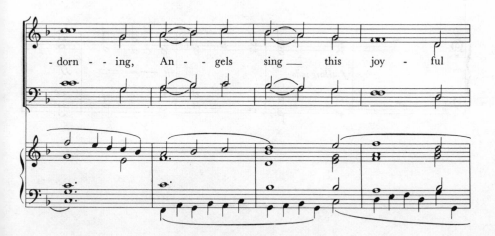

- dorn - - ing,   An - - gels   sing —   this   joy - ful

morn - - ing Peace —— on — earth, —— all — sad - - ness—

scorn - - ing. Born —— to - day —— is Christ— our King.

5. I SING OF A MAIDEN THAT IS MATELESS

15th century

CHARLES F. WATERS

6. KINGS IN GLORY

SELWYN IMAGE   MARTIN SHAW

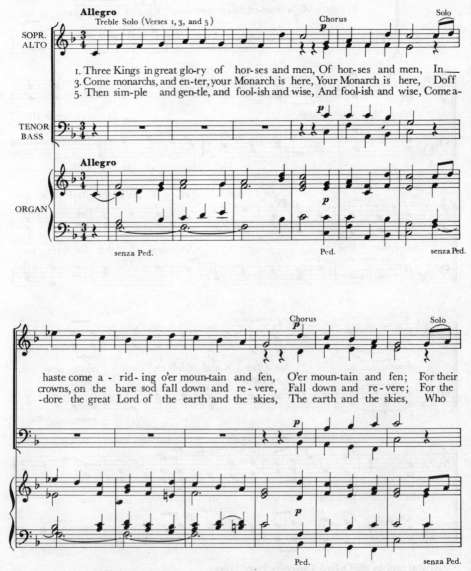

King is a-wait-ing, and lo they would bring, And lo they would bring, The
best you can of-fer is lit-tle, I trow, Is lit-tle, I trow, To the
deigns for us all on this night to be born, This night to be born, This

best of their trea-sure to give to their King, To give to their King.
Lord God of Heav'n you're a-kneel-ing to now, A-kneel-ing to now,
night that is fair-er than mid-sum-mer morn, Than mid-sum-mer morn.

2. Poor shep-herds lie hud-dled to-night on the plain, To-night on the plain, Their
4. Come, shep-herds, and fear not, he will not des-pise He will not des-pise The

sil - ly sheep guard-ing from dan-ger and pain, From dan-ger and pain; For the
gifts that you bring him, tho' rude in men's eyes, Tho' rude in men's eyes. See,—

wolves howl a-round them, and bit - ter the air, And bit - ter the air, That
he's not ar-rayed here in pur- ple and gold, In pur- ple and gold, God's

All fro - - zen and bare.
As lamb —— of your fold.

blows o'er the snow-field all fro - - zen and bare, All fro - zen and bare.
Lamb lies as help-less as lamb —— of your fold, As lamb — of your fold.

7. HERE LIES HE NOW

(HIER LIEG ICH NUN)

Melody and bass by
J. S. BACH
(Ed. Charles Kennedy Scott)

DOROTHY PARRY THOMAS

*To be used if the Air only is sung (as a solo); but better omitted with the four voices.
Copyright, 1945, by the Oxford University Press, London.

8. LORD, FOR THY TENDER MERCY'S SAKE

JOHN HILTON (the elder) d. 1608
(Ed. E.H. Fellowes)

Transposed up a tone, and note values halved. The words are from 'Lydney's Praiers', which form a section of Henry Bull's *Christian Praiers and Holy Meditacions*, 1568. This anthem has been attributed to Richard Farrant, but his name was never associated with it till late in the 18th century. The earlier MSS. agree in ascribing it to the elder John Hilton, of Trinity College, Cambridge, and there is no good reason to doubt that he was the composer. The contrapuntal *Amen* which has sometimes been printed at the conclusion is not found in any text older than the beginning of the 18th century; it was probably first composed and added at about that date.

pp
lives; to de-cline from sin, and in-cline to vir - tue,
lives; to de - cline from sin, and in - cline to vir - tue,
cresc.
lives; to de-cline from sin, and in-cline to vir - tue, that we may
lives; to de - cline from sin, and in - cline to vir - tue, that we may
cresc.
mf
that we may walk in an up-right heart, that we may walk in an
that we may walk in an up-right heart, that we may walk in an
walk in an up-right heart, in an up-right heart, that we may walk in an up-right heart, in an
walk in an up-right heart, in an up-right heart, that we may walk in an up-right heart, in an
2nd time rit. e dim.
up-right heart be - fore thee this day night and ev - er - more. -more.
up-right heart be - fore thee this day night and ev - er - more. -more.
p cresc.
up-right heart be - fore thee this day night and ev - er - more. That we may -more.
up-right heart be - fore thee this day night and ev - er - more. That we may more.

9. AVE VERUM

(JESU, WORD OF GOD INCARNATE)

MOZART

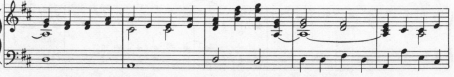

Cleanse us by — the Blood and — Wa - ter Stream - ing from Thy
Cu - jus la - tus per - fo - ra - tum un - da flux - it et

Cleanse us by the Blood and Wa - ter Stream - ing from Thy
Cu - jus la - tus per - - fo - ra - tum un - da flux - it et

Cleanse us by the — Blood and — Wa - ter Stream - ing from Thy
Cu - jus la - tus — per - fo - ra - tum un - da flux - it et

Cleanse us by — the Blood and Wa - ter Stream - ing from Thy
Cu - jus la - tus per - - fo - ra - tum un - da flux - it et

pierc - ed side. Feed us with Thy Bod - y bro - ken, —
san - - gui - ne. Es - to no - bis prae - gus - ta - tum in

pierc - ed side. Feed us with Thy Bod - y bro - ken, —
san - - gui - ne. Es - to no - bis prae - gus - ta - tum in

pierc - ed side. Feed us with Thy Bo - dy
san - - gui - ne. Es - to no - bis prae - gus -

pierc - ed side. Feed us with Thy Bo - - dy
san - - gui - ne. Es - to no - bis prae - gus -

10. WE ADORE THEE, O LORD CHRIST

(ADORAMUS TE, CHRISTE)

VIADANA
Edited and translated by BERNARR RAINBOW

Andante

SOPRANO

We —— a - dore Thee, O Lord Christ,
Ad - - o - ra - mus te, Chri - - - ste,

ALTO

We —— a - dore Thee, O Lord —— Christ,
Ad - - o - ra - mus te, Chri - - - - - ste,

TENOR

We a - dore —— Thee, O Lord —— Christ,
Ad - o - ra - - mus te, Chri - - - - - ste,

BASS

We —— a - dore Thee, O Lord Christ,
Ad - - o - ra - mus te, Chri - - - - - ste,

ORGAN
(for
rehearsal
only)

Andante

we laud —— and bless — Thy ho - ly Name, Thou who by Thy blest
et be - - ne - di - ci - mus ti - - bi, qui - a per san - ctam

we laud —— and bless —— Thy ho - ly Name, Thou who by Thy blest
et be - - ne - di - - ci - mus ti - bi, qui - a per san - ctam

we laud —— and bless —— Thy ho - ly Name, Thou who by Thy blest
et be - - - ne - di - - - ci - mus ti - bi, qui - a per san - ctam

we laud —— and bless —— Thy ho - ly Name, Thou who by Thy blest
et be - - ne - di - - ci - mus ti - bi, qui - a per san - ctam

11. JESU, HOPE OF MEN DESPAIRING

(JESU, UNSER TROST UND LEBEN)

ERNST CHRISTOPH HOMBURG (1659)
Tr: BEATRICE E. BULMAN

Melody anonymous (1714)
Figured bass by J. S. BACH
(Ed. Charles Kennedy Scott)

*To be used if the Air only is sung (as a solo); but better omitted with the four voices.

Copyright, 1950, by the Oxford University Press, London.

piu f

such   tri - um - phant   might   Thou   o'er - cam'st Thy
now   can   harm   no   more   Rage   as   ne'er   he
live   their   joy   dis - play,   Clothe   them - selves   in

piu f

such   tri - um - phant   might   Thou   o'er   cam'st Thy
now   can   harm   no   more   Rage   as   ne'er   he
live   their   joy   dis - play,   Clothe   them - -   selves   in

piu f

such   tri - um - phant might Thou   o'er - cam'st   Thy
now   can   harm   no   more Rage   as   ne'er   he
live   their   joy   dis - play,   Clothe   them - selves   in

piu f

such   tri - um - phant   might   Thou   o'er - cam'st   Thy
now   can   harm   no   more   Rage   as   ne'er   he
live   their   joy   dis - play,   Clothe   them - selves   in

meno f

foes   in   fight.   Break - ing   bars   of   Death's   dark
raged   be - fore.   There - fore   Zi - on   loud   is
gar - ments gay.   Lo,   the   sea   too,   mirth   is

meno f

foes   in   fight. Break - - ing   bars   of   Death's dark
raged   be - fore. There - - fore   Zi - on   loud   is
gar - ments gay. Lo,   the   sea   too,   mirth   is

meno f

foes   in   fight. Break - - ing   bars   of   Death's dark
raged   be - fore. There - - fore   Zi - on   loud is
gar - ments   gay. Lo,   the   sea   too,   mirth is

meno f

foes   in   fight.   Break - ing   bars   of   Death's   dark
raged   be - fore.   There - fore   Zi - on   loud   is
gar - ments   gay.   Lo, — the   sea   too,   mirth   is

meno f

12. GOOD CHRISTIAN MEN REJOICE AND SING

C. A. ALINGTON

ERNEST BULLOCK

Good Christian men re-joice and sing!

Now is the tri-umph of our King! —— To all the world glad news we

songs of vic-to-ry   That Love, that Life which can-not die,

ff (Reeds)   (Reeds)

*)   Ped. ⸱⸱   senza Ped.

mf   poco rall.

And sing with hearts up - lift - ed high: Al - le - lu -

mf   poco rall.

Ped.

UNISON   Più lento   f

- ya !   Thy name we bless, O

f

Allargando   rall.   Più lento

mf (senza Reeds)   cresc.   f

Ped.

*)The Organ may double the voices, if required, throughout these rests - manual only, no pedals used.

To William Lovelock

13. HE IS RISEN

(Two-part)

Mrs. Alexander

CECIL COPE

FULL UNISON

He is ris-en, he is ris-en: Tell it with a joy - - ful

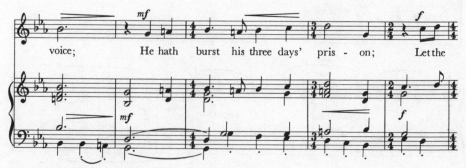

voice; He hath burst his three days' pris-on; Let the

whole wide earth re - joice._____ Death is con - quer'd,

man is free,   Christ has   won___ the   vic - - to -

- ry.

TREBLES   *mp*
Come, ye   sad___ and   fear - ful - heart   - ed,

mf BASSES
Come, ye   sad   and fear - ful - heart - ed,   With glad smile   and

mp a tempo

With— ra - diant brow, Sha-dows have— de - part - ed,

ra - diant brow; Lent's long sha - dows have de - part - ed,

All his woes are o - ver now,

All his woes ——————— are o - ver now, And the

And the Pas- sion he bore: Sin and pain can vex— no more.

Pas - sion — that he bore: Sin and pain can vex— no more.

14. THE STRIFE IS O'ER

18th cent. (?)
Translation by Francis Pott

C. ARMSTRONG GIBBS

Copyright, 1931, by the Oxford University Press, London.

third morn he rose a-gain Glor-ious in maj - es - ty

third morn he rose a-gain Glor-ious in maj - es - ty

third morn he rose a-gain Glor-ious in maj - es - ty

third morn he rose a-gain Glor-ious in maj - es - ty

to reign; O let us swell the joy - - ful

to reign; O let us swell the joy - - ful

to reign; O let us swell the joy - - ful

to reign; O let us swell the joy - ful

strain: Al - - - - - - - le - lu - ya!

strain: Al - - le - lu - ya! - Al - - le - lu - ya!

strain: Al - - - le - lu - ya! Al - le - lu - ya!

strain: Al - - le - lu - ya! Al - - le - lu - ya!

mf

Tranquillo
pp

Lord, by the stripes which wounded thee From death's dread sting thy ser-vants

pp

Lord, by the stripes which wounded thee From death's dread sting thy ser-vants

pp

Lord, by the stripes which wounded thee From death's dread sting thy ser-vants

pp

Lord, by the stripes which wounded thee From death's dread sting thy ser-vants

p

free, That we may live,— and sing to thee: Al-le - lu - - ya! Al -

free, That we may live, and sing to thee: Al-le - lu - - ya! Al - le -

free, That we may live,— and sing — to thee: Al-le - lu - - ya! Al - le -

free, That we may live, and sing to thee: Al-le - lu - - ya! Al -

poco animato

- - le - lu - - ya!   A - - - men.

- lu - - - - ya!   A - - men.

- lu - - - - ya!   A - - men.

- - le - lu - - ya!   A - - men.

rit. al fine

senza Ped.   Ped.

15. ALLELUIA! HEARTS TO HEAVEN

(Unison with descant)

CHRISTOPHER WORDSWORTH
(1807 - 1885)

W. K. STANTON

Al - le - lu - ia! Al - le - lu - ia! Hearts to heaven and

voi - ces raise; Sing to God a hymn of glad - ness,

Sing— to God a hymn of praise; He who on— the

Cross a vic - tim For— the world's sal - va - tion bled,

Je - sus Christ, the King of glo - ry, Now is ri - sen

from the dead.

f (SOPRANOS ONLY)

Christ is ris - en, Christ the first-fruits

senza Ped.

Of the ho - ly har - vest field, Which will all — its

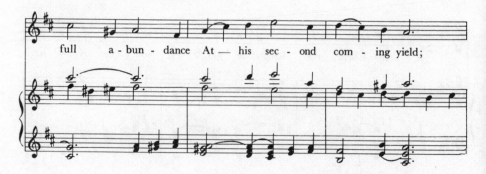

full a - bun - dance At — his sec - ond com - ing yield;

Then the gold - en ears of har - vest Will their heads be -

- fore — him wave, Ri - pened by his glo - rious sun - shine

From the fur - rows of — the grave.

cresc.

cresc.

Ped.

SOPRANOS

Al - le - lu - ia!   Al - le - lu - ia!   Glo - ry be — to

ALL OTHER VOICES

Al - le - lu - ia!   Al - le - lu - ia! Glo - ry be   to

God   on high; —   To the Fa - ther, and   the Sa - viour, Who— has gained the

God   on high;   To   the Fa - ther, and   the Sa - viour, Who— has gained the

vic - to - ry;   Glo - ry to   the Ho - ly Spi - rit, Fount of love and

vic - to - ry;   Glo - ry to — the Ho - ly Spi - rit, Fount of love and

sanc - ti - ty; —   Al - le - lu - ia! Al - le - lu - ia! To   the Tri - une

sanc - ti - ty;   Al - le - lu - ia! Al - le - lu - ia! To   the Tri - une

Ma - jes - ty.   A - - -

Ma - jes - ty.   A - - -

[Ped. Reed   ]

- men.   fff

- men.   fff

16. COME, YE FAITHFUL

St. JOHN DAMASCENE
Tr. J. M. NEALE

R. S. THATCHER

Al - - - - le - lu - - ia!

Thou didst stand, be - stow - - ing That Thy peace which

poco rit.

Al - - - - le - lu - - ia!

ev - er - more Pass - eth hu - man know - - ing.

poco rit.

ff a tempo

fff
molto rit.

17. GIVE LAUD UNTO THE LORD

Melody taken from Richard Langdon's
'Divine Harmony' and ascribed to Keily
Arranged by
ERNEST BULLOCK

Give laud un - to the Lord, ——— from heaven that is so high, Praise him in deed and

18. A CHORAL HYMN

FOR

ADVENT OR ASCENSIONTIDE

Advent words by JOHN MILTON (1608-74)
Ascensiontide words by EDWARD PERRONET (1726-92)
and JOHN RIPPON (1751-1836)

Scottish Melody 'Montrose' (1855)
Arranged by
HENRY G. LEY

Apart from the first note of the 2nd line, which is C in the original, I have preserved the original form of the tune.
This setting may be transposed to the original key of D. This is specially recommended should real trumpets be used.

H.G.L.

err;
fall: Be - fore Him righ - teous - ness shall go, His
Bring forth the roy - al di - a - dem, and

roy - al har - bin - ger.
crown Him Lord of all.

Truth from the earth, like to a flower, shall bud and
Crown Him, ye mar - tyrs of our God, Who from His

*This verse is taken from the Public School Hymn Book.

blos - som then;   and jus - tice from her heaven-ly bower, look
al - tar call;   *Praise Him whose way of pain ye trod, and*

down — on mor - tal men.
crown — Him Lord of all.

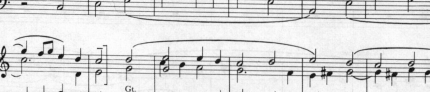

ff (DESCANT)

Rise, God, judge Thou the earth in might, this wick - ed
Ye seed of Is - rael's cho - sen race, ye ran - somed

earth re - dress; for Thou art He who shalt by
of the fall; *Hail Him who saves you by His*

right, the na - tions all pos - sess.
grace, and crown Him Lord of all.

The na - tions all whom Thou hast made, shall
Hail Him, ye heirs of Da - vid's line, whom

come and all — shall frame To bow them low be-
Da- vid Lord did call; *The God in - car - nate—*

Trumpet
Gt.
senza Ped.

fore— Thee Lord, and glo - ri - fy— Thy Name.
Man— Di - vine; and crown Him— Lord— of all.

Trumpet
f
Gt
Ped.

ff
For great Thou art, and won - ders,
Let ev - ery tribe and— ev - ery—
ff

Gt.

19. ABOVE ALL PRAISE AND ALL MAJESTY

MENDELSSOHN

*May be sung unaccompanied

20. ALL PEOPLE AT THIS HOUR

(*KOMMT, SEELEN, DIESER TAG*)

VALENTIN E. LÖSCHER (1713)
Tr. DOROTHY PARRY THOMAS

Melody and figured bass by
J. S. BACH
(Ed. Charles Kennedy Scott)

Con moto e fervore

SOPRANO (or Air) / ALTO / TENOR:
1. All peo-ple at this hour ___ Their hymns of praise are sing-ing, To tell ___ of God's great power ___ New gifts of con-verse
2. All whom God's gift in-spired, ___ The Ho-ly Ghost des-cend-ing, Each word with wis-dom fired ___ All earth-ly speech trans-

BASS:
1. All peo-ple at ___ this hour Their hymns of praise are sing-ing, To tell ___ of Gods ___ great power New gifts of con-verse
2. All whom ___ God's gift ___ in-spired, The Ho-ly Ghost des-cend-ing, Each word ___ with wis-dom fired All earth-ly speech trans-

ORGAN*

*To be used if the Air only is sung (as a solo); but better omitted with the four voices.

21. COME, THOU HOLY SPIRIT, COME

PALESTRINA

1. Come, Thou Ho - ly Spi - rit, come; And from Thy ce - les - tial
Come, Thou Fa - ther of the poor, Come, Thou source of all our

home Shed a ray of light _____ Di - - vine:
store, Come, with - in our bo - - - - - soms shine:

light _____ Di - vine: _____
bo - - - soms shine: _____

2. Thou of com - fort - ers the best, Thou the soul's most wel - come
In our la - bour rest most sweet, Grate - ful cool - ness in __ the

guest, Sweet re - fresh - ment here be - - low;
heat, So - lace in the midst _____ of woe.

here be - low; _____
midst of woe; _____

3. O most bless - ed Light Di - vine, Shine with - in these
Where Thou art not, man hath nought, No - thing good in

bless - - ed Light Di - vine,
art _____ not, man hath nought,

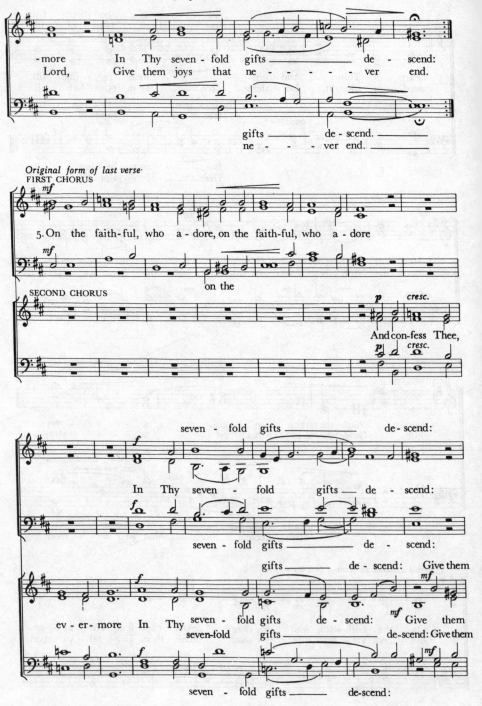

Original form of last verse·
FIRST CHORUS

SECOND CHORUS

Give them Thy sal - va - tion, Lord,   Give them joys that

vir - tue's sure re - ward,   Give them joys— that

dim. e rall.

A - - - men. Al - le - - - lu - - ia.   *pp*

Al - le - - - - - lu - - ia.

nev - - er end.— A - men.

Al - le - - lu - - ia, Al - le - lu - ia.   *dim. e rall.*

Al - le - lu - ia, Al - le - lu - - ia.

nev - - - - - er end. A - men. Al - - le - - lu - - - ia.   *dim. e rall.*   *pp*

nev - - - er end. A - men. Al - le - - lu - - ia.

nev - - er— end.— A - men. Al - - le - lu - ia. ———

nev - - - er end.— A - men. Al - le - - - lu - - ia.   *dim. e rall.*   *pp*

When the last verse is sung in the original form, the four previous verses should be sung by 1st Chorus and 2nd Chorus alternating at the repeats.

22. YE WATCHERS AND YE HOLY ONES

An Anthem on the tune

LASST UNS ERFREUEN

*

Unison and Two-part

with optional four-part harmony

GEORGE OLDROYD

Harmony (optional) | Unison

Al-le - lu - ya, Al-le - lu - ya, Al-le - lu - ya, Al-le - lu - ya, Al-le - lu - - ya!
Al-le - lu - ya, Al-le - lu - ya, Al-le - lu - ya, Al-le - lu - ya, Al-le - lu - - ya!

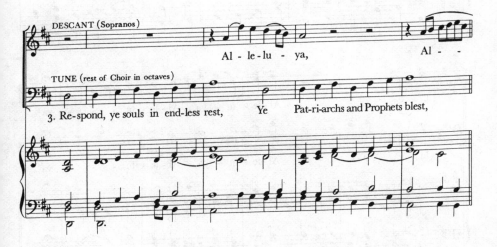

DESCANT (Sopranos)

Al - le - lu - ya, Al - -

TUNE (rest of Choir in octaves)

3. Re-spond, ye souls in end-less rest, Ye Pat-ri-archs and Prophets blest,

- le - lu - ya, Al-le - lu - ya! Al - le - lu - - - -

Al-le - lu - ya, Al-le - lu - ya! Ye ho-ly Twelve, ye Martyrs strong, All

23. PLEASURE IT IS

(Two-part: for Boys only, Men only, or Boys and Men)

W. CORNISH (d.1523)   CECIL COPE

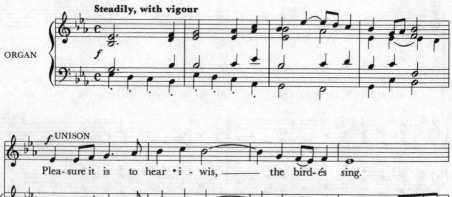

*'in truth'

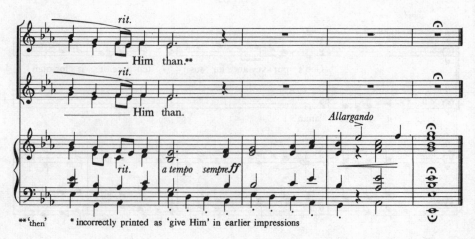

** 'then'   * incorrectly printed as 'give Him' in earlier impressions

24. BLESS THE LORD, O MY SOUL

(Two-part)

Words taken from Psalm civ

C. ARMSTRONG GIBBS

Tempo I, largamente

strength - en-eth man's heart. Bless the Lord, O my

strength - en - eth man's heart. Bless the Lord, O my

strength - en - eth man's heart. Bless the Lord, O my

soul. O — Lord my God, Thou art ve-ry great, Thou art

soul. O — Lord my God, Thou art ve-ry great, Thou art

soul. O — Lord my God, Thou art ve-ry great, Thou art

Allargando

cloth - ed with hon - our and ma - - - jes - ty.

cloth - ed with hon - our and ma - - - jes - ty.

cloth - ed with hon - our and ma - - - jes - ty.

25. THE SOULS OF THE RIGHTEOUS

Wisdom III. 1, 2

STANLEY MARCHANT

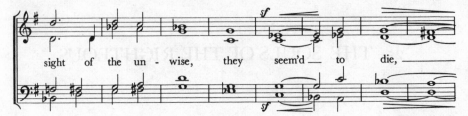

sight   of   the   un - wise,   they   seem'd — to   die, _____

But   they   are _____   in   peace, _____

They _____

But   they

In   peace, _____   they   are   in _____   peace, _____   they

In   peace, _____   they

are   in _____   peace, _____   in   peace. _____

*

26. O THOU WHO AT THY EUCHARIST DID'ST PRAY

W. H. TURTON

MOGENS WÖLDIKE
Based on a melody by KRUGER (1598-1662)

Music reprinted by permission of the composer.

Words from *Hymns Ancient and Modern* by permission.

Copyright, 1954, by the Oxford University Press, London.

done.' Oh, may we all one bread,one bo - dy be,

done.' Oh, may we all one bread,one bo - dy be,

done.' Oh, may we all one bread, one bo - dy be,

done.' Oh, may we all one bread,one bo - dy be,

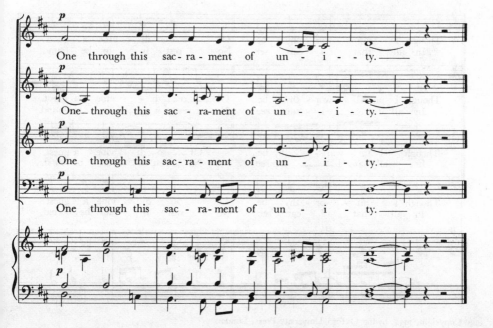

One through this sac - ra - ment of un - i - ty.

One through this sac - ra-ment of un - i - ty.

One through this sac - ra - ment of un - i - ty.

One through this sac - ra-ment of un - i - ty.

27. MY SPIRIT LONGS FOR THEE

J. BYROM
(1692-1763)

JOHN DOWLAND
(Ed. E. H. Fellowes)

Of so di - vine a guest Un-wor-thy though I be, Yet has my
No rest is to be found But in thy bless - ed love; O let my

Of so di - vine a guest Un-wor - thy though I be, Yet has my heart
No rest is to be found But in thy bless-ed love; O let my wish

Of — so di - vine a guest Un-wor-thy though I be, Yet has my heart
No — rest is to be found But in thy bless - ed love; O let my wish

Of so di - vine a guest Un-wor-thy though I be, Yet has my
No rest is to be found But in thy bless - ed love; O let my

heart no rest Un-less it comes from thee, Un-less it comes from thee.
wish be crowned, And send it from a - bove, And send it from a - bove!

— no — rest Un-less it comes from thee, Un-less it comes from thee.
— be — crowned, And send it from a - bove, And send it from a - bove!

— no — rest Un-less it comes from thee, Un-less it comes from — thee.
— be — crowned, And send it from a - bove, And send it from a - bove!

heart no rest Un-less it comes from thee, Un-less it comes from thee.
wish be crowned, And send it from a - bove, And send it from a - bove!

28. O HOLY JESU
(O BONE JESU)

Attributed to PALESTRINA
Edited and translated by BERNARR RAINBOW

Note: In a building with little resonance the pauses may be lengthened
Copyright, 1957, by the Oxford University Press, London.

made   us   thine,   and   hast   re - deem - ed   us,
-a - sti   nos;   tu   re - de - mi - sti   nos

made___ us thine, and_____ hast re - deem - ed   us,
-ā - - sti nos;   tu _____ re - de - mi - sti   nos

made   us   thine,   and   hast   re - deem - ed   us,
-a - sti   nos;   tu   re - de - mi - sti   nos

made   us   thine,   and   hast   re - deem - ed   us,
-a - sti   nos;   tu   re - de - mi - sti   nos

hast   re - deem - ed   us   by   thy most pre - - - - - cious blood.
san - gui - ne   tu - o   prae - ti - o - sis - - - - - si - mo.

hast   re - deem - ed   us   by   thy most   pre - - cious blood.
san - gui - ne   tu - o   prae - - ti - o - - sis - - - si - mo.

hast   re - deem - ed   us   by   thy   most pre - - cious blood.
san - gui - ne   tu - o   prae - ti - - - - o - sis - - si - mo.

hast   re - deem - ed   us   by   thy   most   pre - - cious blood.
san - gui - ne   tu - o   prae - ti - o - sis - - si - mo.

Composed for the Coronation of
Her Majesty Queen Elizabeth II

29. O TASTE AND SEE

Psalm xxxiv, 8

R. VAUGHAN WILLIAMS

This motet may be sung in the key of G flat

Copyright, 1953, by the Oxford University Press, London.

30. YE SERVANTS OF GOD

FESTIVAL HYMN
FOR MASSED SINGING

C. WESLEY
(1745)

Tune: Paderborn (18th cent.)
Arr. by HENRY COLEMAN

Name: The Name all— vic - tor-ious of Je - sus ex - tol: His

King - dom is— glor-ious, and rules ov- er all.

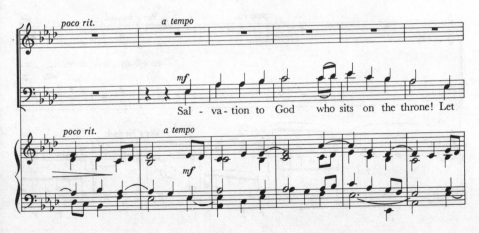

Sal - va- tion to God who sits on the throne! Let

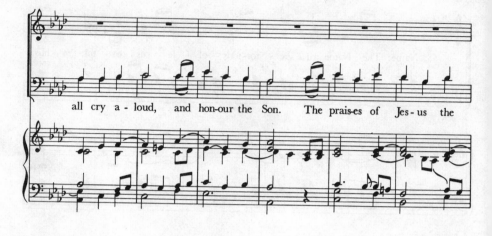

all cry a - loud, and hon-our the Son. The prais-es of Jes - us the

an-gels pro - claim, Fall down on their fac-es, and wor-ship the Lamb.

Then let us a - dore,___ and

give Him His right, All glo-ry and power, all—wis-dom and might, All

hon-our and bless-ing, with an-gels a - bove,— And thanks nev - er—

rall.

ceas-ing, and in-fin-ite love. ——————

rall.   *allargando molto*

31. O, PRAISE GOD IN HIS HOLINESS

(Two-part)

Psalm CL

C. ARMSTRONG GIBBS

This work may be sung in four ways, *(a)* S.A. *(b)* T.B. *(c)* S.A.B. *(d)* S.A.T.B.

32. LET ALL THE WORLD

GEORGE HERBERT   NORMAN GILBERT

*May be sung as a unison, two-or three-part anthem.

Copyright, 1947, by the Oxford University Press, London.

King!   The Heav'ns are not too high,   His praise may thi - ther fly;   The earth is not too low,   His prais - es there may grow.   Let   all   the   world ___   in   ev - 'ry   cor - ner

*If sung as a unison anthem, these four bars should be sung by all voices.

33. O LORD, I WILL PRAISE THEE

Isaiah, Chapter 12

GORDON JACOB

senza Ped.

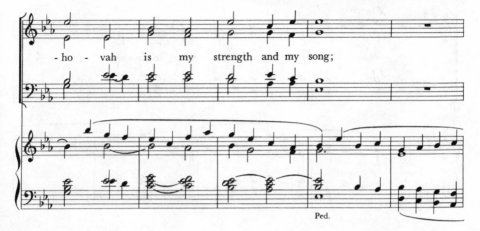

-ho - vah   is   my   strength and my song;

Ped.

he al-so is be - come my sal - va - tion. _____

cresc.

ff

Praise — the Lord, call up-on his name, de-clare his do - ings a-

-mong the peo - ple, make men-tion that his name is ex-

alt - - - ed.

things: this is known in all the earth.   Cry out   and

shout,   thou in - hab - i - tant of   Zi - on: for great   is the

Ho - ly one of Is - ra - el   in   the midst   of   thee.

To my wife

34. ALL FROM THE SUN'S UPRISE

A metrical paraphrase of the 100th Psalm

(S.A.B.)

GEORGE SANDYS
(1578-1644)

PHILIP TOMBLINGS

All from the sun's up-rise Un-to his set-ting rays, Re-sound in ju-bi-lees The great Je-ho-vah's praise. Him

serve a - lone: In — tri-umph bring Your gifts   and   sing ————   Be - fore His

throne.

Man drew from man his birth; But God   his   no - ble   frame   Built   of the

35. HELP ME, O LORD

Canon

THOMAS ARNE

This Canon is printed here in its original key.   It may be transposed up or down.

36. COME, SWEETEST DEATH

(KOMM, SÜSSER TOD)

Anonymous (1725)
Tr: BEATRICE E. BULMAN

Melody and figured bass by
J. S. BACH
(Ed. Charles Kennedy Scott)

*To be used if the Air only is sung (as a solo); but better omitted with the four voices.
Copyright, 1945, by the Oxford University Press, London.

37. FLOCKS IN PASTURES GREEN ABIDING

(from Cantata No. 208)

Translation by
PHYLLIS JAMES

J. S. BACH
Arranged for four voices by
STANLEY ROPER

Man. I Flute 8 ft.
Man. II Soft Swell
Ped. 8 and 16 ft.

In this Edition, entries of the flutes are marked 'Fls.' and their endings //

—Safe - ly, safe - ly— with their Shep - herd rest.

cresc.

mf

Ped.

rit.
(2nd time rit. molto)

p   mf   p

Fine a tempo   cresc.   mp
      p

(Omit this bar
first time) With the food of life He feeds them, To the— fold He

p

Fine a tempo
      ff

p   cresc.

mp

sen. Org.

Ped.

38. FORGET ME NOT
(VERGISS MEIN NICHT)

GOTTFRIED ARNOLD (1697)
Tr: DOROTHY PARRY THOMAS

Melody anonymous (1698)
Figured bass by J. S. BACH
(Ed. Charles Kennedy Scott)

1. 'For-get me not!' Then shall I not per-mit Thee To be for-got, Oh ho-ly stem of Jes-se.
2. Safe from all harms, My Shepherd and my Mas-ter, With-in Thine arms Thou bear-est me to pas-ture.

*To be used if the Air only is sung (as a solo): but better omitted with the four voices.

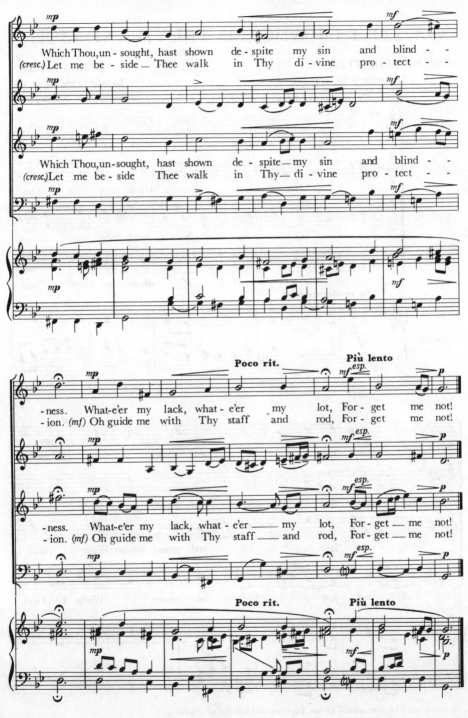

Which Thou, un-sought, hast shown de-spite my sin and blind-
(cresc.) Let me be-side Thee walk in Thy di-vine pro-tect-

Which Thou, un-sought, hast shown de-spite my sin and blind-
(cresc.) Let me be-side Thee walk in Thy di-vine pro-tect-

Poco rit. **Più lento**

-ness. What-e'er my lack, what-e'er my lot, For-get me not!
-ion. (mf) Oh guide me with Thy staff and rod, For-get me not!

-ness. What-e'er my lack, what-e'er my lot, For-get me not!
-ion. (mf) Oh guide me with Thy staff and rod, For-get me not!

Poco rit. **Più lento**

39. O LOVE OF WHOM IS TRUTH AND LIGHT

JOHANN SCHEFFLER (1624-77)
tr. Catherine Winkworth

FINN VIDERÖ
Based on a melody of 1539
(Adapted by Temple Bevan)

40. BE PEACE ON EARTH*

(Two-part)

BISHOP HEBER

WILLIAM CROTCH
Arranged by Henry G. Ley

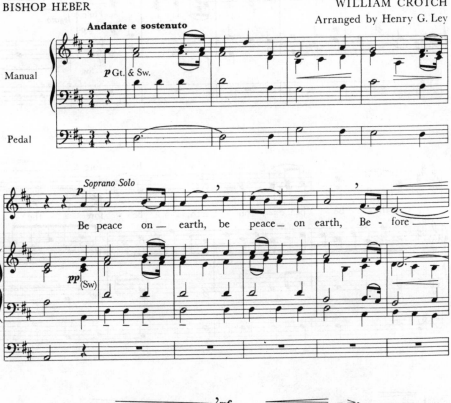

*From the Oratorio 'Palestine'

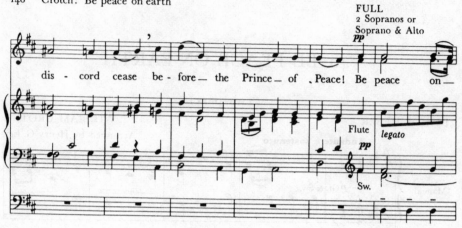

FULL
2 Sopranos or
Soprano & Alto

dis - cord cease be - fore — the Prince — of ˏPeace! Be peace on —

Flute   legato

Sw.

earth, — be peace — on earth, Be - fore — the

Be - fore

Prince, the Prince— of Peace: Mes - si - - ah — comes,— let

fu - rious dis - - cord cease — be - fore — the Prince — of

Peace!— Be peace on — earth, be peace on — earth, Dis -

- ease and anguish feel His blest con - trol, And woe no more dis -

-turb the troubled soul,— the trou - bled— soul! My beams of glad-ness

all   our hearts il - lume,   all   our hearts il - lume,   And

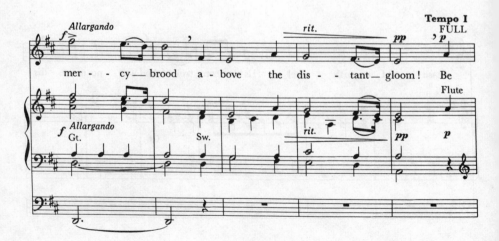

mer - - cy— brood a - bove   the dis - - tant— gloom!   Be

peace on — earth, be peace — on earth, Be - fore — the

Prince, the Prince — of Peace, Mes-si - - ah — comes, — let

fu - - rious dis - - cord cease, be - fore — the Prince — of

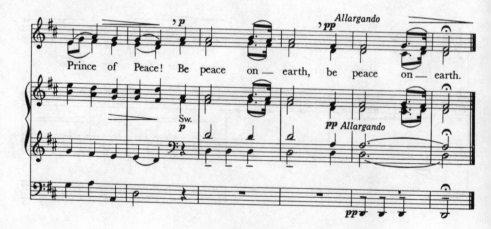

41. JESU, THE VERY THOUGHT OF THEE

T. L. de VICTORIA

But sweet-er far Thy face ____ to see, sweet-er far Thy ____

__ But sweet - - er far Thy face ____ to see, sweet - er far Thy face to

But sweet - - er far Thy__ face ____ to see, sweet - er far Thy__ face to

But sweet-er far Thy face to see, Thy face to

face to ____ see, and in Thy__ pre - - sence rest, and in Thy pre-sence rest.

see, and ____ in Thy pre - - sence, pre - sence rest, and in Thy pre - sence rest.

see, and in Thy pre-sence, in Thy pre - sence rest, and in Thy pre - sence rest.

see, to see, and in Thy pre - - sence rest.

42. ABOVE HIM STOOD THE SERAPHIM

(Two-part)

RICHARD DERING
(Ed. Stanley Roper)

43. HE THAT IS DOWN NEEDS FEAR NO FALL

JOHN BUNYAN

JOHN DOWLAND
(Ed. E. H. Fellowes)

44. MOST GLORIOUS LORD OF LIFE

(S.T.B. or S. Bar. B.)

EDMUND SPENSER
(c. 1522-99)

WILLIAM H. HARRIS

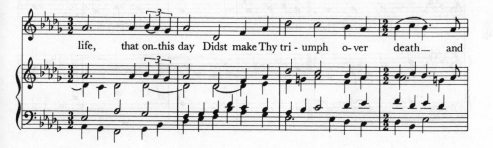

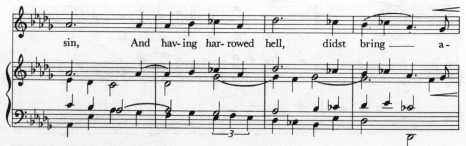

Words from *Songs of Praise*
Copyright, 1932, by the Oxford University Press, London.

-way Cap - ti -vi - ty thence cap- tive, us —— to win.

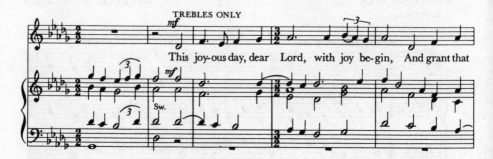

TREBLES ONLY

This joy-ous day, dear Lord, with joy be-gin, And grant that

we for whom Thou did - dest die, Be - ing with Thy dear blood clean

washed   from sin, May live for ev- er in fe - li - · ci-

45. VOX ULTIMA CRUCIS

(TARRY NO LONGER; TOWARD THINE HERITAGE)

(Unison)

JOHN LYDGATE
(1370? - 1447)

WILLIAM H. HARRIS

It is suggested that this be sung twice–first as a Solo, or by a few voices, then as a full (Unison) Chorus, the small notes being sung by voices of lower range.

Tar-ry no lon - ger; t'ward thine he - ri - tage

Haste on thy way, and be of right good cheer. Go each

day on-ward on thy pil-grim-age; Think how short time thou shalt a - bide

The old English has been modernised, but 'bigg'd above the starres clear' and 'most entere' (entire) have been retained.

W. H.H.

here.   Thy place is   bigg'd a-bove the star-res clear,   None earth-ly

pal   ace wrought   in   so state-ly wise.   Come on, my   friend, —

— my   bro-ther most   en - tere!   For thee I   of-fer'd my blood —

— in   sac - ri-fice.   Tar-ry no

46. MY EYES FOR BEAUTY PINE

(Unison: optional SATB)

ROBERT BRIDGES   HERBERT HOWELLS

My eyes — for beau-ty pine, — My soul — for God-dës grace; No oth-er care_ nor hope is mine, To heaven I turn — my face. —

One splen - - dour thence is shed —

— from all —— the stars a - bove: 'Tis nam- ed when God's

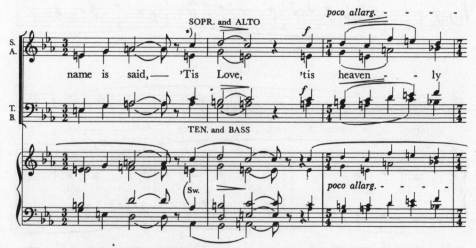

SOPR. and ALTO
*)
name is said, —— 'Tis Love,   'tis heaven - ly

TEN. and BASS

poco allarg. - - - -

*)When sung entirely in unison, only the Soprano part to be sung here and in the next three bars.
The small notes to be played on the organ.

Love._ And ev -

- - ery gen-tle heart —— that burns — with true de - sire, Is

lit from eyes— that mir-ror part of that ce - les - - - tial fire.—

47. DROP DOWN, YE HEAVENS

(Two-part)

Isaiah XLV. 8
Psalm LXXXV. 10. 11.

HEATHCOTE STATHAM

right-eous-ness spring up   to - geth - er.

Mer - cy and truth   are met   to - geth-er: right-eous-ness and

peace have kissed each   oth-er.   Truth   shall flour-ish

*The G is essential; the lower voices can, if necessary, sing the optional Eb.
**If the compass of the organ does not extend to top C, a 4ft. stop only will be needed here.

48. RICHARD DE CASTRE'S PRAYER TO JESUS

CAROL A.D. 1430

Set to music in the
Dorian Mode by
SIR R.R. TERRY

eek— with— thought.——— Jhe - su, in whom is
I — schulde do. ——— Jhe - su,— keepe them

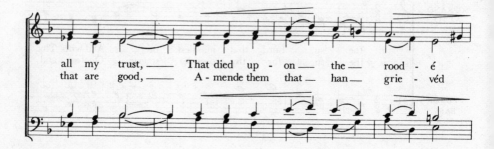

all my trust,—— That died up - on— the— rood - é
that are good,—— A - mende them that— han— grie - véd

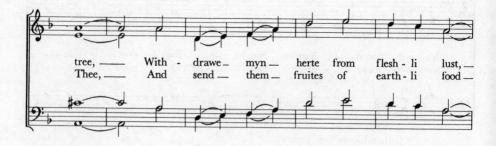

tree,—— With - drawe— myn— herte from flesh - li lust,—
Thee,—— And send— them— fruites of earth - li food—

—— And from all world - ly—— van - y - - té. ———
cresc. As each man need - eth— dim. in his de - gree.——

To Mrs. D. R. Marlowe and the Dudden Hill Girls' School Choir

49. A PRAYER OF ST. RICHARD OF CHICHESTER

(Unison with descant)

L. J. WHITE

clear - ly,   love thee more dear - ly and fol - - low

thee   more near - ly,

Solo

p

Ped.

and fol - - low thee   more near - - ly.

FULL CHORUS *mf*

O   ho- ly

pp

Gt. *mf*

to F. F.

50. O HOW AMIABLE

The words taken from
Psalms 84 and 90

R. VAUGHAN WILLIAMS

O how a‑mi‑able are thy dwell‑ings: thou Lord ——— of

Bless-ed are they that dwell in thy— house:—— They will be

al - way prais-ing   thee. ———

The glo-rious Ma-jes-ty   of— the— Lord our God be up-on us:——

pros-per thou the work of our hands up-on us.

O pros-per thou our han-dy-work, O

pros - per thou our han-dy - work.

O   God,   our

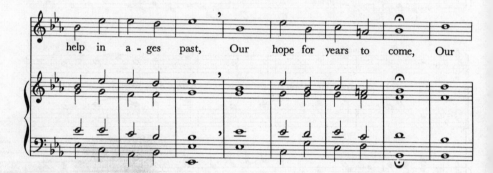

help   in   a - ges   past,   Our   hope   for   years   to   come,   Our

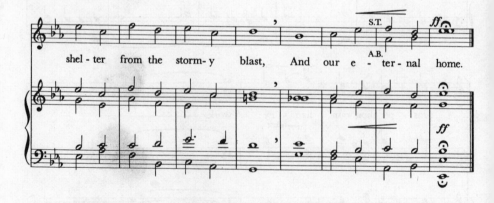

shel - ter   from   the   storm - y   blast,   And   our   e - ter - nal   home.